INCREDIBLE CREATURES OF THE Indian Ocean

Learn About Animals Including Clownfish, Blue Whales, Yeti Crabs, and the Giant Clam!

Nicole K. Or

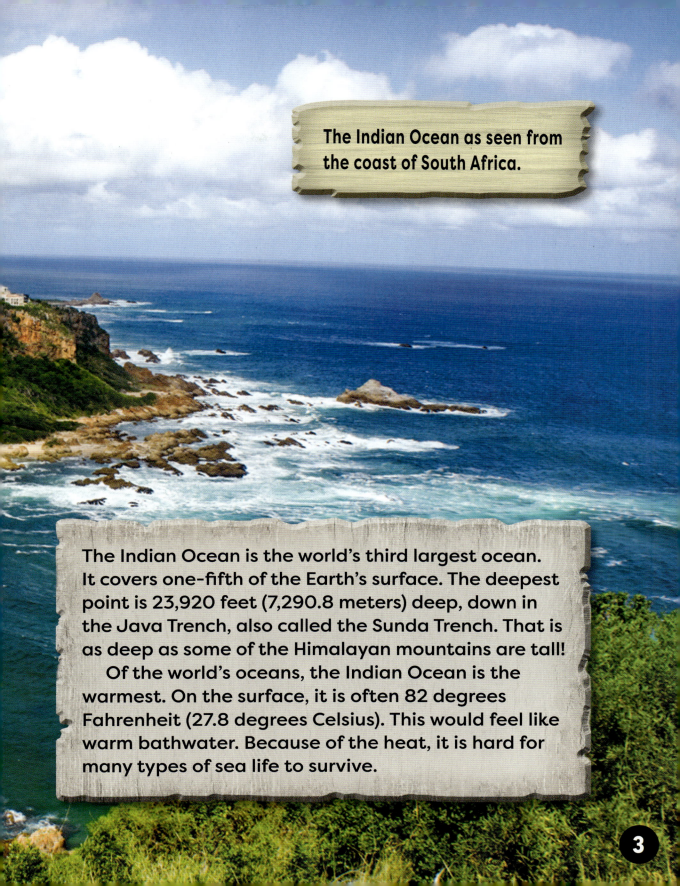

The Indian Ocean as seen from the coast of South Africa.

The Indian Ocean is the world's third largest ocean. It covers one-fifth of the Earth's surface. The deepest point is 23,920 feet (7,290.8 meters) deep, down in the Java Trench, also called the Sunda Trench. That is as deep as some of the Himalayan mountains are tall!

Of the world's oceans, the Indian Ocean is the warmest. On the surface, it is often 82 degrees Fahrenheit (27.8 degrees Celsius). This would feel like warm bathwater. Because of the heat, it is hard for many types of sea life to survive.

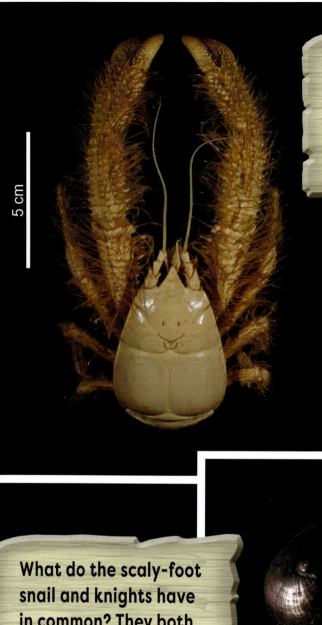

The yeti crab was discovered in 2005. The hair on its claws helps the yeti crab harvest bacteria to eat.

What do the scaly-foot snail and knights have in common? They both wear armor! This snail's shell is made out of iron.

Some creatures like the water hot. From vents on the ocean floor, superheated water provides food and warmth for many unusual creatures. Fuzzy yeti crabs, transparent sea cucumbers, scaly-foot snails, and other unusual deep sea creatures are found only near these hydrothermal vents.

The Indian Ocean has 57 groups of islands. Saunder's tern is a seabird that nests on these islands. They hover over the water for long periods of time. Once they've chosen a meal, they quickly plunge down to catch insects, fish, crabs, or mollusks.

The Saunder's tern drinks lots of water, but they only drink when flying. They dip low to the water and plunge their heads in for a cool drink.

Madagascar (mad-a-GAS-kar) is the largest island in the Indian Ocean. Off the coast of Madagascar and along other Indian Ocean coasts, you'll find beautiful, colorful coral reefs. When most people look at corals, they think they're looking at plants, but corals are actually animals. Corals are polyps (PAH-lips), tiny sea creatures that live in colonies (KAH-luh-nees). The reefs they build are home to many types of fish and other sea life.

The zebra shark is just one of the many fish that love life around the coral reef. During the day, they rest on the seafloor. At night, they hunt for food.

The Indian Ocean is one of the best places to spot sea turtles. The leatherback sea turtle is the planet's largest turtle. It can grow up to 6 feet (1.8 meters) long and weigh up to 2,000 pounds (907.2 kilograms). It is the only sea turtle that doesn't have a bony shell. It has a leather-like covering instead.

The hawksbill turtle is named for its sharply pointed head, which looks like a bird's beak. When this turtle is born, its shell is heart-shaped.

The giant clam lives on coral reefs and on the seafloor. This mollusk (**MAH-lusk**) can reach up to 4 feet (1.2 meters) long and weigh more than 500 pounds (226.8 kilograms). Once they find a spot to grow, giant clams do not move for the rest of their lives. This makes them easy prey for eels, snails, and sea stars.

You might think giant clams all look alike, but in fact, every giant clam shell is different from the next.

People used to think giant clams caught food by snapping their shell shut. This isn't true. Giant clams can't actually close their shells.

The Indian Ocean is where you'll find the common clownish. They are usually bright orange and have white stripes with thin black outlines. Clownfish are able to live in sea anemones, which usually sting and poison animals. The sea anemones protect the clownfish from predators while the clownfish clean the anemones and provide food. All clownfish are born male. If the lead female in a social group dies, the lead male can become a female clownfish.

Another type of clownfish in the Indian Ocean is the maroon clownfish. They are also called spine-cheeked anemonefish since they have spines on their cheeks and live in anemones. These are the largest type of clownfish in the world. They grow to over 6 inches (15.2 centimeters) long.

Another fish living in the Indian Ocean is the ornate ghost pipefish. It looks like a weedy stick, which lets it blend in and hide around coral reefs. It will drift along in the water without moving at all to stay hidden from predators.

Ghost pipefish are related to seahorses. They usually float with their long mouths facing down so they can suck up tiny crustaceans.

The regal blue tang is a type of surgeonfish that lives in small groups. It helps corals by eating algae that might choke coral growth. In some parts of the Indian Ocean, regal blue tangs have yellow bellies.

There are many types of colorful angelfish and surgeonfish in the coral reefs of the Indian Ocean. Emperor angelfish adults are bright yellow, orange, and blue and have stripes. If they become frightened, they can create knocking sounds.

The Indian Ocean is full of sharks. The wobbegong (WAH-bee-gong) is a carpet shark that lives on the seafloor. This shaggy shark waits for prey to swim by, then its mouth opens wide and swallows it. It can also creep along the bottom, using its fins like feet. It will sneak up on a crab, lobster, or octopus, then pounce.

The cookiecutter shark lives near islands. It is also called the cigar shark because its body is long and narrow. The belly of this shark glows! This helps it blend in with the moonlight. It also helps attract bigger fish. Cookiecutter sharks bite these larger fish to get a meal. Sometimes, the fish escapes with a cookie-shaped wound that will later heal.

The cookiecutter shark regularly replaces its teeth like other sharks. Its special bottom teeth are shed and replaced in one full row at a time!

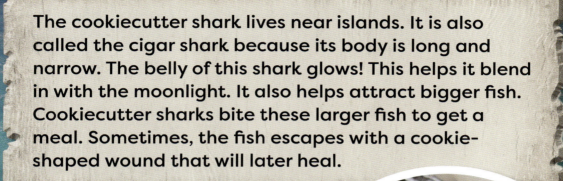

One of the most gentle creatures that lives in the Indian Ocean is the dugong (DO-gong). They are totally vegetarian. Dugongs are related to manatees, but they have longer snouts and a tail that is more like a dolphin's. Dugongs can live up to 70 years. Dugong mothers only have a few babies in their lives, devoting many years to raising each baby.

Dugongs have a very big upper lip, which they use to eat seagrass off the bottom of the ocean. This is why they're nicknamed "sea cows."

The blue whale, the largest animal on earth, swims in oceans around the world, including the Indian Ocean. They grow up to 98 feet (29.9 meters) long and weigh up to 200 tons (181.4 metric tons). Just a blue whale's tongue weighs as much as an elephant!

There are many types of whales in the Indian Ocean. Humpback whales are easy to spot because they have bumps around their mouths and on their heads called "tubercles." Humpback whales are very active on the surface of the ocean, breaching (coming out of the water) and slapping the water with their fins and tails. Scientists think they could be playing or communicating!

The Indian Ocean is home to many types of albatross. These are some of the largest flying birds on earth. The wandering albatross, also known as a snowy albatross, has the largest wingspan of any bird—their wings can spread up to 11 feet (3.4 meters) wide. That's almost as large as a small car! They travel long distances around the world, staying in the air for many hours without having to flap their wings.

The black-browed albatross is another type of albatross you might see in the Indian Ocean. Like other albatross babies, their chicks are born with soft downy feathers.

One of oddest creatures in the Indian Ocean is the peacock mantis shrimp. These brightly colored shrimp have special limbs called "dactyl clubs" that move 50 times faster than you can blink! They deliver fast, deadly punches to stun their prey. They've even been known to break glass in private aquariums.

The wide, warm Indian Ocean is home to so many amazing, beautiful, and sometimes strange creatures.

Peacock mantis shrimps have eyes that move separately from one another. They can also see many more colors than humans can.

FURTHER READING

Books

Callery, Sean. *Life Cycles: Ocean*. New York: Kingfisher, 2011.

Curnick, Pippa, and Jen Feroze. *Let's Explore . . . Ocean!* Oakland, CA: Lonely Planet Kids, 2016.

Hughes, Catherine D. *National Geographic Little Kids First Big Book of the Ocean*. Washington, DC: National Geographic Children's Books, 2013.

Kainen, Dan, and Carol Kaufmann. *Ocean: A Photicular Book*. New York: Workman Publishing Company, 2014.

Oachs, Emily Rose. *Indian Ocean*. Minnetonka, MN: Bellwether Media, 2016.

Spilsbury, Louise, and Richard Spilsbury. *Indian Ocean*. Portsmouth, NH: Heinemann, 2015.

Web Sites

NASA's Climate Kids: Ocean
https://climatekids.nasa.gov/search/ocean/

National Geographic Kids—Ocean Facts
https://www.natgeokids.com/uk/discover/geography/general-geography/ocean-facts/

Science Kids—Fun Ocean Facts
https://www.sciencekids.co.nz/sciencefacts/earth/oceans.html

GLOSSARY

colony (KAH-luh-nee)—A group of animals of the same kind that live in an area.
coral (KOR-ul)—A stony underwater polyp.
dugong (DO-gong)—A vegetarian marine mammal that is one of the most gentle creatures in the Indian Ocean.
Madagascar (mad-a-GAS-kar)—The largest island in the Indian Ocean.
mollusk (MAH-lusk)—A sea animal with a soft body, no bones, and usually a hard outer shell.
polyp (PAH-lip)—A small ocean creature with a tube-shaped body and tentacles around its mouth.
predator (PREH-dih-tur)—An animal that hunts other animals for food.
prey (PRAY)—An animal that is hunted for food.
reef (REEF)—A large group of coral.
sea anemone (SEE uh-NEH-muh-nee)—An underwater animal that stays in one spot and looks like a flower.
trench (TRENCH)—A very deep cut in the seafloor.
wobbegong (WAH-bee-gong)—A type of carpet shark that lives on the seafloor.

PHOTO CREDITS

pp. 2–3—Vaiz Hai; pp. 4–5—Alamy/Science History Images; p. 4 (top inset)—Noémy MOLLARET, (bottom inset)—Kentaro Nakamura, et al.; pp. 6–7—Shutterstock/Vinod Pillai; p. 7 (inset)—Shutterstock/DHANYA G; pp. 8–9—Shutterstock/Ong.thanaong; p. 9 (inset)—Shutterstock/dade72; p. 11 (inset)—Shutterstock/Abdul Razak Latif; pp. 14–15—Kurit afshen; p. 15 (inset)—Vojce; pp. 16–17—Shutterstock/Joe Belanger; p. 17 (inset)—Shutterstock/John Back; pp. 18–19—Shutterstock/Greens and Blues; p. 18 (inset)—Shutterstock/chonlasub woravichan; p. 21 (inset)—Shutterstock/JSUBiology; pp. 22–23—Shutterstock/Ivanenko Vladimir; p. 23 (inset)—Shutterstock/Andreas Wolochow; pp. 24–25—Shutterstock/Jonas Gruhlke; p. 24 (inset)—Shutterstock/Ajit S N; pp. 26–27—Shutterstock/stylefoto24; p. 27 (inset)—Shutterstock/David Osborn; pp. 28–29—Shutterstock/Gerald Robert Fischer; p. 29 (inset)—Shutterstock/DiveSpin.Com. All other photos—Public Domain.

INDEX

Albatross 26–27
Black-browed albatross 27
Blue whales 24–25
Clownfish 14–15
Cookiecutter shark 21
Coral reefs 8–9, 12, 16, 18, 19
Dolphins 22
Dugongs 22–23
Emperor angelfish 18–19
Ghost pipefish 16–17
Giant clam 12–13
Hawksbill turtle 11
Humpback whales 25
Hydrothermal vents 5
Java Trench 2, 3
Leatherback turtle 10–11
Madagascar 8
Maroon clownfish 15
Mollusks 6, 12–13
Ornate ghost pipefish 16–17
Peacock mantis shrimp 28–29
Polyps 8
Regal blue tangs 18
Saunder's tern 7
Scaly-foot snail 4, 5
Sea anemones 14
Sea cucumbers 5
Sea turtles 10–11
Seahorses 17
Snowy albatross 26
South Africa 3
Spine-cheeked anemonefish 15
Sunda Trench 3
Wandering albatross 26
Wobbegong shark 20–21
Yeti crab 5
Zebra shark 9

© 2025 by Curious Fox Books™, an imprint of Fox Chapel Publishing Company, Inc.

Incredible Creatures of the Indian Ocean is a revision of *Water Planet: Life in the Indian Ocean*, originally published in 2018 by Purple Toad Publishing, Inc. Reproduction of its contents is strictly prohibited without written permission from the rights holder.

Paperback ISBN 979-8-89094-174-9
Hardcover ISBN 979-8-89094-175-6

Library of Congress Control Number: 2024950036

To learn more about the other great books from Fox Chapel Publishing, or to find a retailer near you, call toll-free at 800-457-9112 or visit us at *www.FoxChapelPublishing.com*.
You can also send mail to:
Fox Chapel Publishing
903 Square Street
Mount Joy, PA 17552

We are always looking for talented authors. To submit an idea, please send a brief inquiry to acquisitions@foxchapelpublishing.com.

Fox Chapel Publishing makes every effort to use environmentally friendly paper for printing.

Printed in China